ANIMAL
BABIES

illustrated by Estella Hickman
written by Dandi

Some animals, like albatrosses, geese, swans, and penguins, mate for life and raise animal babies.

A baby albatross is called a *fledgling*.

Baby geese are called *goslings*. The day
after they hatch, goslings swim in a
straight line, with Dad in front,
Mom in back.

A baby swan is called a *cygnet*. It takes a cygnet 3-4 years to grow up completely into a beautiful swan.

Male penguins carry eggs on their feet. After the eggs hatch, the fathers carry the *chicks* on their feet for several weeks.

Chick is what we call a baby chicken. But a baby turkey is a *poult*.

Out of the largest egg
in the animal kingdom
comes another *chick*.

The baby ostrich can run
off with its parents soon
after it hatches.

Animals may have any
number of babies. The Koala
bear has one *cub* every other year,
then carries it on her back for another year!

Kangaroos have one baby, called a *joey*.
The joey is carried around for about seven
months in the mother's pouch.

The 9-banded armadillo always has four babies.

Who holds the record for most living babies? The tailless tenrec, with 31!

The male Darwin frog keeps about 20 eggs in his throat until they hatch. Then he coughs up a batch of tiny *froglets!*

Horses have newborn *foals*. If it's a boy, it's called a colt. But if it's a girl, it's a *filly*.

Cats have *kittens*. But so do rabbits. Rabbit *kits* are born in complicated burrows under the ground.

Baby beavers are called *kits* or *pups*. Beavers raise their babies in a lodge, with underwater entrance and exit.

Most of us know dogs have *puppies*. But other animals have babies called *pups* too.

Dog and pup

Fox and pup
(or cub)

Wolf and pup

Baby seals are called *pups*.

Seals can roar, growl or purr.

A *calf* is a baby cow. But it may also be a baby camel, dolphin, elephant, giraffe, or whale.

A *cub* may be a baby bear...a baby lion...a baby
cheetah...a baby tiger.

And what about a *kid*?

It could be a goat. It might
be an antelope.

Or, you never know.

A *kid* might just be a kid.

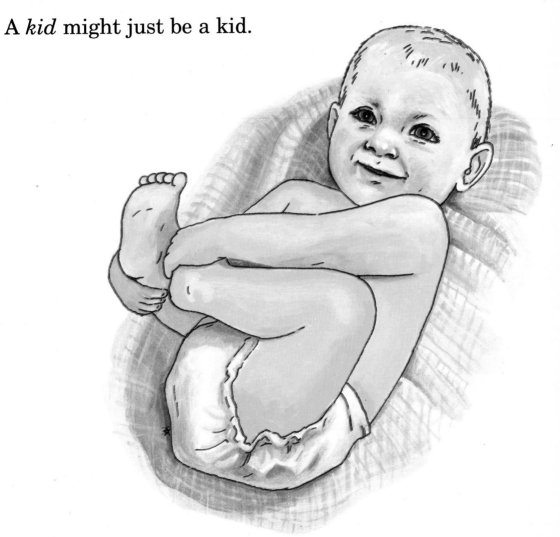